COUNTRIES OF THE WORLD

Ukraine

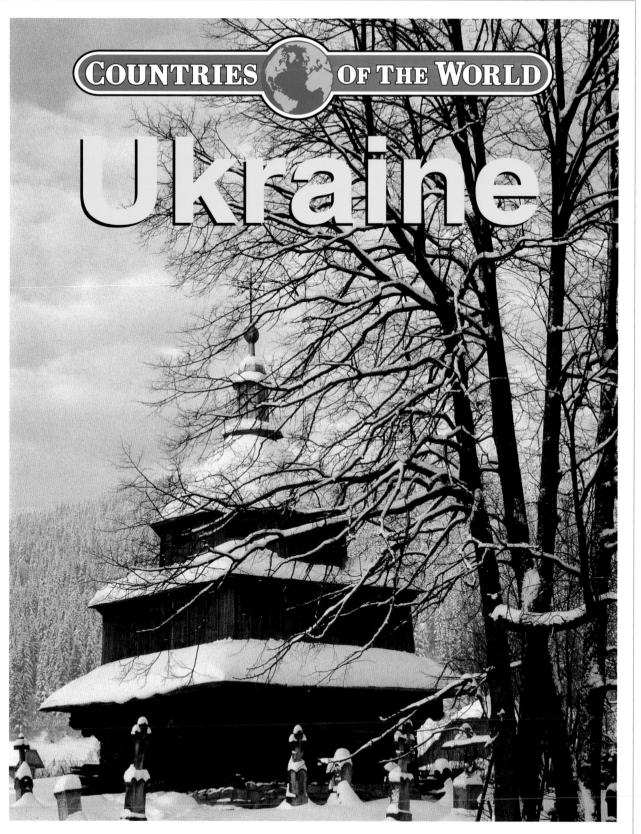

Gareth Stevens Publishing
A WORLD ALMANAC EDUCATION GROUP COMPANY

About the author: Pavel Zemliansky was born and raised in Ukraine. After graduating from college, he worked as an English teacher and translator before moving to the United States. He teaches writing to college students and writes his own travel and academic articles for publications. He travels to Ukraine at least once a year to visit his family and friends.

Written by
PAVEL ZEMLIANSKY

Edited by
RICHARD DAVIES

Edited in the U.S. by
MONICA RAUSCH

Designed by
ROSIE FRANCIS

Picture research by
SUSAN JANE MANUEL

First published in North America in 2002 by
Gareth Stevens Publishing
A World Almanac Education Group Company
330 West Olive Street, Suite 100
Milwaukee, Wisconsin 53212 USA

Please visit our web site at
www.garethstevens.com
For a free color catalog describing
Gareth Stevens Publishing's list of high-quality
books and multimedia programs, call 1-800-542-2595
or fax your request to (414) 332-3567.

© **TIMES MEDIA PRIVATE LIMITED 2002**
Originated and designed by
Times Editions
An imprint of Times Media Private Limited
A member of the Times Publishing Group
Times Centre, 1 New Industrial Road
Singapore 536196
http://www.timesone.com.sg/te

Library of Congress Cataloging-in-Publication Data
Zemliansky, Pavel.
Ukraine / by Pavel Zemliansky.
p. cm. — (Countries of the world)
Summary: Presents information on the geography, history, government, economy, people, social life and customs, arts, contemporary issues, and relations with North America of Ukraine, a country in Eastern Europe that regained its independence from the Soviet Union in 1991.
Includes bibliographical references and index.
ISBN 0-8368-2355-9 (lib. bdg.)
1. Ukraine—Juvenile literature. [1. Ukraine.] I. Title.
II. Countries of the world (Milwaukee, Wis.)
DK508.515.Z46   2002
947.7—dc21   2001057767

Printed in Malaysia

1 2 3 4 5 6 7 8 9 06 05 04 03 02

PICTURE CREDITS
A.N.A Press Agency: 4, 6, 9, 25, 34, 84
Art Directors & Trip Photographic Library: 3
    (center), 11, 18, 24, 36, 41, 47, 53, 56, 85
Jan Butchofsky/Housterstock: 57, 67
Tania D'Avignon: 1, 2, 3 (top), 3 (bottom),
    7, 8, 10, 15 (top), 16, 17, 20 (bottom), 29,
    31, 32, 33, 38, 39, 40, 42, 45, 46, 50, 51,
    52, 58, 59, 60, 61, 62, 63, 64, 65, 66, 68,
    69, 70, 71, 72, 74, 76, 77, 79, 83, 90, 91
Focus Team — Italy: 21, 28, 54
Getty Images/Hulton Archive: 12, 13, 20
    (top), 27, 75, 78, 80, 81, 82
Haga Libary, Japan: 73
HBL Network Photo Agency: 43, 55
The Hutchison Library: cover, 5, 14, 19, 22,
    23, 30, 35
NewsPix: 48, 49
Topham Picturepoint: 15 (bottom), 26, 37, 44

Digital Scanning by Superskill Graphics Pte Ltd

Contents

AN OVERVIEW OF UKRAINE

Ukraine is a country in Eastern Europe that regained its independence from the Soviet Union in 1991. This move toward independence was the most successful effort by Ukrainians to be free of foreign rule. Because of Ukraine's strategic position near the eastern boundary of Europe, throughout history Ukrainians have fought attempts by other, more powerful peoples and nations to take control of their country. Over the centuries, Ukraine has been under the control of the Mongol Golden Horde, Lithuania, Poland, Russia, and, finally, the Soviet Union.

Despite considerable mineral, industrial, and agricultural resources, the early years of independence have not delivered the prosperity that many Ukrainians have hoped for.

Opposite: **The onion-shaped domes of an Eastern Orthodox church in Yalta are typical of Ukraine's impressive churches.**

Below: **Ideal land for farming makes agriculture a dominant industry in Ukraine.**

THE FLAG OF UKRAINE

The Ukrainian flag consists of two horizontal stripes of equal width. The top is blue; the bottom is yellow. The colors symbolize the sky and golden fields of Ukraine. First displayed in 1848, the flag was suppressed as Ukraine was conquered by foreign rulers. The blue and yellow flag reappeared after the country's independence.

Ukraine's national emblem is the trident, known as the *tryzub* (tree-ZOOB). Many theories relate to its origins. In medieval times, it was thought the trident represented the division of the world into three spheres: the earthly, the celestial, and the spiritual, as well as the union of the three natural elements of air, water, and earth.

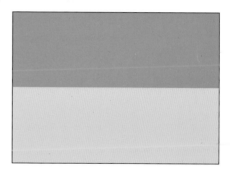

Geography

Ukraine is located in the eastern part of central Europe between Poland and Russia. In the west, the country borders Poland, Slovakia, and Hungary. In the southwest, Ukraine shares borders with Moldova and Romania. In the north, its neighbor is Belarus (formerly a Soviet republic known as Belorussia). In the east and northeast lies Ukraine's largest neighboring country and former ruler — Russia.

The territory of Ukraine is 233,089 square miles (603,700 square kilometers), making it the second-largest country on the continent of Europe. Two seas border Ukraine: the Black Sea in the south and the Sea of Azov in the southeast.

The Crimean Peninsula is a prominent part of Ukraine. It juts out into the Black Sea in the southern part of the country and is attached to the mainland by the narrow Perekop Isthmus. Crimea's geography includes mountains, grasslands, and a narrow coastal plain.

THE UKRAINIAN RIVIERA
Considered by many to be the "Ukrainian Riviera," the Crimean Peninsula is home to some of Ukraine's most picturesque spots. The area is a top destination for holiday travelers, and its warm climate is ideal for growing fruit and producing wine.
(A Closer Look, page 66)

Below: Flat, fertile grasslands called steppes cover much of Ukraine's landscape.

Left: **The Dnipro River, seen here in the Ukrainian capital of Kiev (also known as Kyiv), is the country's main waterway.**

Mountains and Plateaus

Ukraine's landscape mainly consists of fertile level land called steppes. Parts of western Ukraine, however, are crossed by the Carpathian Mountains. These scenic mountains stretch into Poland, Slovakia, and Romania and abound in fascinating flora and fauna. The tallest peak in the Ukrainian Carpathians is Mount Hoverla, which is 6,762 feet (2,061 meters) high.

The other exception to the generally flat landscape of Ukraine is the Crimean mountain range on the Crimean Peninsula in the south. In geological terms, the Crimean Mountains are younger than the Carpathians and are still forming, so they are rockier and steeper than the Carpathians. The Carpathian Mountains attract skiers and hikers in winter; the Crimean range is popular with rock climbers.

Rivers and Lakes

Ukraine's rivers and streams total 154,100 miles (247,947 km) in length. Ukraine's main river is the Dnipro (also known as the Dnieper), which flows from north to south through the country. The Dnipro is 1,367 miles (2,200 km) long, with approximately 609 miles (980 km) flowing through Ukraine. Other rivers include the Dniester, the Southern Buh, the Pripyat, and the Desna. The mouth of the Danube River borders southern Ukraine, linking it to western Europe.

The largest bodies of fresh water in Ukraine are man-made lakes created through the building of dams on rivers. The Dnipro's lakes include the Kakhovka, Kiev, and Kremenchuk reservoirs.

Climate

Ukraine's geographic position may conjure up images of extreme cold, with lots of snow and freezing winters, but most areas of Ukraine have four distinct seasons, with temperatures fluctuating between very hot in summer and sometimes very cold in winter. Winter temperatures range from cool in the south to below freezing inland. Summers are generally warm or hot throughout the country. Western Ukraine and the Carpathians, however, are generally cooler than the rest of the country in summer.

Located in the northern interior of the country, Kiev has an average temperature of 21° Fahrenheit (-6° Celsius) in January, the coldest month. In July, the warmest month, the average temperature is 68° F (20° C). On the Crimean Peninsula's southern coast, at the southern end of Ukraine, the average temperature in January is 39° F (4° C). In July, the average temperature is 75° F (24° C). In the southern region of Ukraine, winters are usually mild and rainy. Frequent snowfalls in the Carpathian Mountains make the mountains a skiers' paradise in the winter months of February and March.

Below: **Winter snows cling to a church in the Carpathians in western Ukraine.**

Plants and Animals

Above: **The Askaniya-Nova Nature Reserve on Ukraine's southern steppe is home to animals such as the European bison.**

Some areas of eastern Ukraine are heavily wooded, especially with oak and maple trees. In this part of the country, tall, straight poplars are planted in rows along the highways and on the edges of fields for protection from winds. Moving farther west, toward the capital Kiev, the scenery changes. Oaks and maples give way to pine and fir trees. In the Carpathian Mountains, in western Ukraine, elm and pine trees are most common. These mountain areas are heavily wooded and full of wildlife. The thickest oak and maple woods are found in the northern part of the country.

In the south, particularly in Crimea, vegetation is sparse because of the hot and dry climate. Most of Crimea's landscape consists of low, thin shrubs with virtually all arable land on the southern coast occupied by vineyards and peach orchards.

Wildlife in Ukraine includes elk, deer, and wild pigs. Bison and wild horses have long been extinct in the wild and can only be seen in national parks. Other species, such as the mouflon (wild sheep), spotted deer, and muskrat have been successfully reintroduced into their natural habitats in Ukraine. A network of nature and wildlife refuges has been set up to protect Ukraine's animal life, especially the beaver, lynx, elk, and muskrat.

History

Early Settlers of Ukraine

Two of the most developed early cultures, in what is now Ukraine, were the Trypillia civilization and the culture of the ancient Scythians.

The Trypillians (4000–2000 B.C.) thrived in western and central Ukraine. Archaeological evidence shows that the Trypillia culture was mainly agricultural: its people lived on wheat, barley, and other crops.

Scythians (c. 800–c. 200 B.C.) were nomadic tribes that inhabited southern regions of eastern Europe and parts of Asia. They were a warlike people, famous for elaborate golden artifacts and large and mysterious stone statues of women, known as *babas* (BAH-bahs). The Scythians were succeeded by the Sarmatians.

Ukraine experienced a procession of rulers after A.D. 200. The Goths arrived from the Baltics and were replaced by the Huns in 375, followed by the Bulgars and Avars in the fifth and the sixth century. From the seventh to the ninth century, much of Ukraine was home to the Turkic Khazars and, later, the Magyars.

POTTERY FROM THE PAST

Ukraine has a long history of ceramics, starting with the first settlers of Ukraine and continuing through the centuries. Opishnya and Hutsul are two styles of pottery Ukrainians produce today.

(A Closer Look, page 60)

Left: **Built by the Scythian nomadic tribes, stone babas have survived centuries in the Ukrainian countryside.**

Kiev and the Kievan Rus

Ukraine's greatest ancient civilization was the Kievan Rus (also Kyiv Rus), which flourished from the ninth to the thirteenth century. Kiev, the current capital of Ukraine, was also capital of this medieval state. Both Ukrainians and Russians believe that this kingdom was the ethnic and cultural cradle of their peoples.

Although Kievan Rus was a monarchy, its various rulers consulted with a public assembly called a *veche* (VAY-chay) when making decisions. The veche's powers varied from city to city, but it could accept or reject any new ruler. By controlling a city's military force, the veche could stop a ruler's plans for war.

Late Medieval Ukraine

In the thirteenth century, the center of Ukrainian political and social life moved to the western part of the country as part of the kingdom of Galicia.

Ukrainian Galicia's most prominent ruler was Prince Roman (1201–1264), who built strong ties with the neighboring empires of Hungary, Lithuania, and Poland. During his reign, western European influences on Ukrainian politics and culture increased.

Above: The Kyevo-Pecherska Lavra monastery is a lasting monument of the Kievan Rus kingdom.

KIEV: CRADLE OF UKRAINIAN CIVILIZATION

Kiev is the modern-day capital of Ukraine, but its history dates back more than 1,500 years, when it was the center of the medieval state of Kievan Rus — an ancient kingdom that has a special place in Ukrainian culture and history.

(A Closer Look, page 52)

11

Foreign Rulers

By the fourteenth century, Ukraine was controlled by three different powers — Lithuania, Poland, and the descendants of the Mongol tribes. The strengthening of ties between Poland and Lithuania led to the Union of Lubin in 1569, a treaty through which Poland annexed Lithuanian-ruled areas of Ukraine. For the next century, ethnic Ukrainians were influenced by Polish political and cultural developments. Mongol influence was limited to Crimea.

In 1648, Kozak leader Bohdan Khmelnytsky (1595–1657) asked the Russian Empire for help in overthrowing Polish rule. Ukrainians, however, ended up exchanging one foreign ruler for another. From the seventeenth to the early twentieth century, much of Ukraine was part of the Russian Empire. Russian governments suppressed and often prohibited Ukrainian culture and language. A Ukrainian peasant was a serf, or *kripak* (kree-PAHK). Serfdom continued until 1861, when, in an effort to modernize Russia, the Russian czar passed a law freeing the serfs.

Above: In the 1918 Treaty of Brest-Litovsk, Russia recognized the independence of a number of countries, including Ukraine, but the treaty was abolished at the end of World War I, and Ukraine remained under Russian control.

KOZAKS: WARRIOR RACE

Kozaks (koh-ZAHKS) — also known as Cossacks — hail from the banks of the Dnipro River. Kozaks are known throughout history for their bravery and were used by various rulers of Ukraine as mercenary soldiers.

(A Closer Look, page 54)

The Ukrainian National Republic

The Russian Revolution in February 1917 allowed freedom of speech and lifted restrictions on minorities in Ukraine, and Ukrainians began forming their own government. In April 1917, historian and intellectual Mykhaylo Hrushevsky (1866–1934) was elected president, and in 1918 the Ukrainian National Republic was formed. The republic, however, was short-lived. Civil war soon raged in Ukraine as the Bolshevik Red Army, the supporters of the former Russian imperial rulers, and Ukrainian nationalists fought for control of the region.

Under Soviet Rule

In 1922, Ukraine became one of fifteen Soviet Socialist Republics that made up the Soviet Union. Collectivization of farms and industrialization led to a famine in 1932–33, during which an estimated five to seven million Ukrainians died. Millions more Ukrainians died during the battles of World War II. The reemergence of Ukrainian nationalism during German occupation in World War II was quickly stamped out by Soviet authorities as they reclaimed Ukraine.

Below: **Ukrainian villagers watch the devastation of the countryside during World War II. Nazi Germany and the Soviet Union fought many of their battles on Ukrainian soil.**

Independence

After nearly seventy years of Communist Party rule as part of the Soviet Union, the breakup of the Soviet Union allowed the Ukrainian parliament to declare Ukraine's independence on August 24, 1991. This decision was met with mixed reactions. The nationalist-minded citizens were enthusiastic about the independence for Ukrainian people. Ethnic Russians in Ukraine, however, were worried that political separation from the former Soviet republics would lead to the discrimination of non-Ukrainian minorities in Ukraine.

Since independence, Ukraine has achieved political recognition from other nations. Ukraine is a member of the United Nations (U.N.), the Council of Europe, and the Organization for Security and Co-operation in Europe. Ukraine has participated in peacekeeping missions in the former Yugoslavia, as well as in other international projects.

Reforms to Ukraine's economy have moved slowly, as the government battles inflation and poor industrial performance.

Above: Demonstrators in downtown Kiev wave the Ukrainian flag defiantly as they call for independence from the Soviet Union in 1990.

Princess Olga (890–969)

Olga was the widow of Igor I, prince of Kiev (c. 877–945), and the grandmother of Prince Vladimir I (956–1015). In 945, while attempting to collect excessive taxes, her husband was assassinated by his subjects. Because their son was too young to rule, Olga served as ruler of the kingdom of Kievan Rus from 945–964. She had her husband's murderers scalded to death and hundreds of their followers killed. Olga became the first royal Kievan to adopt Christianity and was canonized as the first saint of the Russian Orthodox Church.

Princess Olga

Bohdan Khmelnytsky (1595–1657)

The leader of the Zaporozhzhian Kozaks, Bohdan Khmelnytsky organized a rebellion against Ukraine's Polish rulers in 1648. Supported by Crimea's Tatars, Khmelnytsky's actions won the support of Ukrainians and led to a mass uprising against the ruling Poles. Forced to make peace, Poland agreed to an independent Kozak state within Ukraine. War broke out again in 1651, but Khmelnytsky was unable to repeat his previous successes. At the 1654 Pereyaslav Agreement, Khmelnytsky sought help from the Russian Empire, pledging his Kozaks' allegiance to the Russians, who later invaded Poland. The Russians gradually took control of Ukrainian lands and continued to rule the region until 1917.

Stepan Bandera (1909–1959)

The name of Stepan Bandera is constantly associated with the idea of Ukrainian nationalism. Bandera was the leader of the Organization of Ukrainian Nationalists in the 1930s and 1940s. During World War II, he and his guerrilla army fought both Soviet and Nazi German authorities. Bandera considered both groups enemies of Ukraine. He was killed in 1959 in Munich, Germany, allegedly by agents of the Soviet secret police, the KGB. Bandera was considered a traitor by the Soviets for fighting against the Soviet rule of Ukraine during the war. Since Ukraine's 1991 independence, Bandera's life and legacy have been reexamined, although he continues to be a highly controversial figure.

Stepan Bandera

Government and the Economy

The Structure of the Ukrainian State

Ukraine is a democratic republic. The head of state is the president, who is elected for a five-year term. Each president is allowed a maximum of two terms. The lawmaking, or legislative, branch of the government is the Verkhovna Rada (Supreme Council). Made up of 450 members, the Verkhovna Rada — Ukraine's parliament — is elected for a term of four years.

The president appoints a prime minister and deputy prime ministers, who are approved by the Verkhovna Rada. Members of parliament and the president are elected by public vote.

Ukraine is divided into twenty-four *oblasti* (OB-lahs-tee), or regions, and the autonomous republic of Crimea. As an autonomous republic, Crimea is allowed to make many political and economic decisions.

Below: Ukraine's parliament is democratically elected and meets in Kiev.

Left: The novelty of democratic elections in Ukraine is reflected in the large turnouts for political rallies.

Economic Reforms

The Ukrainian government announced that Western-style free-market reforms in the economy were its top priority following independence in 1991. As part of the Soviet Union, Ukraine had many plants, factories, and farms, but they were poorly managed and inefficient. The Ukrainian government's privitization programs and economic reforms aimed to make industries more productive, and the country and its people more prosperous.

The government introduced a new currency, *hryvnia* (HRIV-nyah), in 1996 and an aggressive anti-inflation program. Inflation dropped to about 2 percent a month, but because the government was no longer completely subsidizing consumer prices, the cost of living grew, and the gap between the rich and the poor widened. Inflation has averaged about 20 percent per year since 1998.

THE POLITICS OF YOUTH

Young Ukrainians have been at the forefront of politics in the short time that the country has been independent. Demonstrations forced the government on two occasions to change unpopular policies, and youth organizations continue to campaign on various issues.

(A Closer Look, page 58)

Mineral Resources

Ukraine's main natural resource is coal, which is mined in the Donets Basin in the eastern part of the country. Small deposits of oil and natural gas are also found in Ukraine, but the country depends mainly on imports for these resources. Most oil fields are located in western Ukraine with a few in the center of the country. Other natural resources present in Ukraine include manganese, iron ore, nickel, sulfur, and titanium.

Below: **Metals are heated to make alloys at a metalurgical works near Dnipropetrovsk.**

Industrial Production

The Donets Basin in eastern Ukraine has become the country's industrial heartland because the area has large deposits of mineral resources. Mining and transportation equipment, as well as heavy machinery and chemical products are produced in the region. The large number of factories and processing plants have made the Donets Basin densely populated and today the area is one of the world's most comprehensive metallurgical and heavy industrial complexes.

Ukraine is a large steel producer and also manufactures machine tools, tractors, railroad locomotives, and aircraft. Mining is an important industry, and agricultural, textile, and food processing industries also have a large presence in Ukraine.

CHERNOBYL'S NUCLEAR CATASTROPHE

The name Chernobyl will be forever associated with the worst nuclear accident in history. The explosion at the nuclear power plant forced the evacuation of thousands of people, and the effects of radioactive contamination are still felt today.

(A Closer Look, page 44)

Agriculture

Ukraine was once referred to as the breadbasket of Europe because of the volume and quality of its agricultural production. The quality of the country's black soil is so great that Ukraine has the capacity to supply much of the European continent with food.

Ukraine's major agricultural products are wheat and sugarbeets. The country also produces barley, oats, rye, millet, buckwheat, and rice. Other crops include corn and potatoes.

Homegrown Produce

The Crimean Peninsula has long been famous for its vineyards and wines. The central and eastern regions of the country have many apple and cherry orchards. Most Ukrainians like to grow their own fresh fruits and vegetables in an attempt to be self-sufficient, especially people who live in the country and in villages, where many houses have small plots of land near them to grow food.

During the Soviet Union era, agricultural production and the raising of animals was concentrated into large-scale collective and state farms. Recent agricultural restructuring has allowed private households to develop their own small-scale gardening, fruit growing, and livestock operations.

Above: **A mechanical harvester simplifies the work that Ukrainian farmers have been doing for centuries.**

People and Lifestyle

Regional Differences

Ethnic Ukrainians constitute 73 percent of the population, and ethnic Russians make up 22 percent. The remaining minorities belong to other ethnic groups, such as Belorussians, Poles, Crimean Tatars, and Romanians.

The various regions of Ukraine have significant ethnic, cultural, and linguistic differences. The most noticeable difference is the distinction between the mostly Russian-speaking east and Ukrainian-speaking west. Traditionally, because of the geographical closeness to Russia, eastern parts of Ukraine have been influenced by the Russian language and culture. Here, street and store signs are usually written in Russian, and Russian can be heard in the streets more often than Ukrainian. The eastern region

THE CRIMEA'S MUSLIM TATARS

One ethnic and cultural minority attracting much attention in recent years is the Muslim Crimean Tatars (*above*), who were forcibly moved to Central Asia and Siberia by the Soviet Union dictator Joseph Stalin in the 1940s and 1950s. In the early 1990s, the Tatar people began to return to Crimea, reviving their culture and language. They are building new mosques, houses, and cultural centers. In addition, the Crimean Tatars have established their own media and political organizations and are represented in the Crimean and Ukrainian parliaments.

Left: A Ukrainian's appearance reflects the mixed heritage of a people living at the crossroads of Europe.

Above: **Two women meet for a chat in the Ukrainian countryside.**

also has many Russian-language schools, universities, newspapers, and television and radio stations. As well as Russian, most people in the east also speak Ukrainian fluently.

In the west, Ukrainian is the predominant language, but many people know Polish and Hungarian, as well as Russian. Mass media in both Ukrainian and Russian are popular in western areas.

City Attractions

The most populated areas of Ukraine are around Kiev and the eastern part of the country, near the industrial Donets Basin. Kiev is Ukraine's largest city with a population of over 2.5 million people. Kiev's population has been expanding because a number of professionals have moved to the capital from other parts of the country in search of better jobs. Other large cities include Dnipropetrovsk, Donets'k, and Kharkov in the east; L'viv in the west; and Simferopol in the south. The populations of these cities range from several hundred thousand to over one million people.

Family Life

Ukrainian families are relatively small; it is rare for a family to have more than two or three children. Deteriorating economic conditions since independence have meant a drop in the birthrate.

Both parents in a Ukrainian family usually work, not only for economic reasons, but also because of a long-standing cultural tradition that discourages women from staying at home and depending financially on their husbands. While the parents are at work, young children are usually cared for at day care centers. To begin receiving the government-provided retirement pension, men can retire at the age of sixty, while women can stop working at the age of fifty-five.

Ukrainian city dwellers usually occupy a small apartment in a high-rise complex. A family of four usually lives in a two-bedroom apartment with a living room and a kitchen. Villagers traditionally live in more spacious detached houses that are usually built of brick, with a tile or metal roof. Most houses have plots of land to grow fresh fruits and vegetables.

VILLAGE LIFE

Many Ukrainians are choosing to move to cities in search of jobs, but villages still have an important part to play in the country's culture. Villagers treasure and preserve old customs and values, ensuring that traditions are passed on to future generations.
(*A Closer Look, page 70*)

Left: **Ukrainian families, either in the city or countryside, usually have only two or three children.**

Above: **Kiev's Besarabska Market is similar to many Ukrainian markets.**

Shopping

Most Ukrainians prefer to shop for food at markets, which are found both in cities and in the country. Markets are popular because they offer lower prices than stores and because food at the market often is fresher. Some markets have sections that sell inexpensive clothes and housewares as well.

When Ukrainians go to the market to buy food, they prefer to buy enough for the whole week ahead. Small day-to-day food purchases are usually made in grocery stores, which can be found everywhere, both in large cities and in small towns and villages. These popular grocery stores usually go by the name of *hastronom* (hahs-troh-NOHM). Hastronom customers usually go to three different counters to select, pay for, and collect their purchases.

Ukraine's larger cities have Western-style supermarkets that sell prepackaged foods and department stores containing clothes and household items. With the development of a free-market economy, many elegant and expensive shops that sell clothes, electronics, and gifts have sprung up in the country's big cities. Most villages have a general store that sells a variety of goods.

Education

The Ukrainian educational system is currently being reformed. Since independence, schools throughout the country have begun to emphasize Ukrainian history, language, and culture.

All Ukrainian children attend school from the age of six or seven. In 2001, Ukraine introduced a twelve-year system of compulsory education. Completion of a high school education allows students to attend a university or college. Vocational schools cover high school subjects and professional training and allow graduates to get jobs in their chosen professions or continue their studies at a college.

Private schools began to appear in Ukraine after the start of the free-market reforms in the 1990s, but most schools are still run by the state. Before the beginning of the economic reforms, elementary, secondary, and higher education in Ukraine was free and financed by the government. Now, private schools and many of the country's universities and colleges charge their students for tuition. While low compared to the prices of private schooling in Western countries, the fees are above what many Ukrainian families are able to afford.

The school year begins on September 1 and ends in late May or early June. In addition to a long vacation in summer, students have five- to ten-day breaks in fall, winter, and spring.

To enter a university or a college, a Ukrainian high school graduate must take entrance examinations. Ukraine has no national entrance test, and colleges and universities may have different entrance requirements. All universities require students to take an oral or written Ukrainian language exam.

A course of higher education usually lasts five years. Graduates are awarded a diploma of higher education. Some universities and colleges have four-year courses that allow students to graduate with a bachelor's degree, which is a less advanced degree than the diploma of higher education.

Almost every large Ukrainian city has a university and several specialized colleges, called institutes. These specialized institutes include engineering, medical, and arts institutes. Some of the best-known universities are those in Kiev, Kharkov, and L'viv.

Below: **Students have a university or institute to choose from in most Ukrainian cities. These students attend Kyiv Polytechnic Institute.**

Country of Many Religions

Throughout Ukraine, churches dominate the landscape. They have many different styles and sizes, including traditional churches with onion-shaped domes and modern large cathedrals.

The most popular Christian denominations in Ukraine are Ukrainian Orthodox under a Moscow or Kiev patriarch; Ukrainian Autonomous Orthodox; Greek, or Eastern Rite, Catholic; and Roman Catholic. The first two denominations have more followers in the eastern and central parts of the country, while Catholicism is well represented in the western region.

The Baptist, Pentecostal, and Evangelical churches are fast-growing Christian communities in Ukraine. The Muslim and Jewish faiths are also present.

Above: **Eastern Orthodox religious followers in Ukraine are divided among a church headed by a Moscow patriarch, a church headed by a Ukrainian patriarch, and the Ukrainian Autonomous church.**

During the Soviet era, religion, along with Ukrainian language and culture, was discouraged by the communists. The communist Soviets wanted to build a society without ethnic, cultural, and religious distinctions. Many church leaders were imprisoned or exiled, and churches were closed.

Religious Revival

Religion in Ukraine today is separated from the state by law, but religious organizations play an increasingly important role in the country's social life. They run some schools and raise money for various charities. Religious leaders are a common sight at large public gatherings, such as political rallies and demonstrations.

More Ukrainians have become aware of religious issues as social conditions have changed in the country. In June 2001, Pope John Paul II visited Ukraine for the first time. One of the highlights of the five-day visit was the blessing of the country's new Catholic university in L'viv.

Left: **Catholic clergy pray at a service in L'viv conducted by Pope John Paul II during his first visit to Ukraine in June 2001.**

Language and Literature

Ethnic Identity

The issue of language is very important in modern Ukraine after centuries of Russian domination. Because Ukraine has been independent for only just over a decade, language influences not only cultural and intellectual life but also the political climate. Many Ukrainians, especially those in the nationalist camp, see allegiance to the Ukrainian language as allegiance to the country itself. Preference for Russian can sometimes be interpreted as lack of patriotism. Most Ukrainians, however, are fluent in both Ukrainian and Russian. Russian language and culture are still taught in Ukraine's schools and at its universities.

Ukrainian belongs to the Eastern Slavic (Slavonic) group of languages and is closely related to Russian and Belorussian. Despite its similarities to these languages, the Ukrainian language's distinct grammar, vocabulary, and phonetic systems make it a separate language rather than a dialect of other Slavic languages. Ukrainian also borrows from Tatar and Turkish, which were introduced when Ukraine was occupied by these cultures in

Left: **This telephone booth is painted in Ukraine's national colors. Although Ukrainian shares the same Cyrillic lettering, it is completely separate from similar Slavic languages, such as Russian.**

medieval times. For example, the Ukrainian word for watermelon is *kavun* (kah-VUN). Borrowed from Tatar, it is not similar to the word for watermelon in other Slavic languages. The Ukrainian word *maidan* (maj-DAN), which means "square" or "a place for public gatherings," is of Turkish origin and also cannot be found in any other Slavic language.

As in Russian, Belorussian, and Bulgarian, Ukrainian uses the Cyrillic alphabet, which received its name from one of its inventors — the Macedonian monk Saint Cyril.

Literary Favorites

Ukrainian poet Taras Shevchenko (1814–1861) is not only honored in Ukraine, but is also well known abroad. His patriotic poetry, aimed at ending the cultural and political oppression of the Ukrainian people, inspired generations of Ukrainians.

Works by novelist Mykhaylo Kotsyubynsky (1864–1913) are considered fine examples of European modernism at the beginning of the twentieth century. Poets Ivan Franko (1856–1916) and Lesya Ukrayinka (1871–1913) are known for their lyrical, patriotic works. Franko also wrote prose about his native western Ukraine, while Ukrayinka created plays based on folk themes.

Arts

Ukrainian art is a mixture of rich folk traditions and mainstream European forms. Throughout history, Ukrainian artists, musicians, and painters have developed ingenious ways of blending folk motifs, stories, and characters into their art, creating original forms to appeal to various audiences. Interest in Ukrainian arts and culture has increased in recent years, both in Ukraine and abroad.

SOROCHINTSY'S FAIRGROUND ATTRACTIONS

The small town of Sorochintsy plays host to one of Ukraine's oldest and most vibrant celebrations — the Sorochintsy Fair. The fair attracts tens of thousands of people to its cultural and commercial events.
(A Closer Look, page 64)

TRAVELING MUSICIANS

Kobzari (kob-zah-REE) were traveling musicians and singers who played stringed musical instruments called *kobza* (KOB-zah), which later developed into a more modern instrument (*left*) known as a *bandura* (bahn-DOO-rah). Ukraine's oldest and most honored folk instrument, the kobza's status in Ukrainian folk music is similar to the status of the guitar in Spain or bagpipes in Scotland. All kobzari were blind. The musicians traveled from village to village led by guides, playing their music and singing their songs for a living. Their repertoire consisted of religious, folk, and historic songs.

Left: **Dressed in national costume, Ukrainians perform a folk dance. Professional groups attract large audiences.**

Song and Dance

Ukrainians are known throughout the world for their folk songs and dances. Professional song and dance ensembles are popular in Ukraine and often attract large audiences at concerts and festivals. Many Ukrainians perform in amateur song and dance groups in their spare time. People invited to a Ukrainian wedding, birthday, or family reunion might be asked to join in for a group song or dance.

One of the country's premier professional folk ensembles is the Kiev-based Veryovka Ukrainian Folk Choir. The choir consists of both a singing group and a dancing group that perform folk songs and dances, as well as songs by contemporary Ukrainian composers. The choir tours extensively in Ukraine and all over the world.

When it comes to pop music, most young Ukrainians prefer to listen to Western performers, but talented Ukrainian pop musicians always attract large audiences. Among Ukraine's homegrown attractions are the pop band Vopli Vidoplyasova, also known as VV, and singer Iryna Bilyk, who is a major female star in the Ukrainian music industry.

DANCES OF THE SOUL

Fast or slow, Ukrainian folk dances are full of character, portraying the legends, customs, and traditions of the country. The dances vary from region to region, with different moves, content, costumes, and accompanying music.
(A Closer Look, page 46)

Theater

All large Ukrainian cities have professional theater companies that stage a variety of plays, ranging from Shakespeare to experimental works by modern authors. Many of these cities, such as Kharkov, have both a Russian and a Ukrainian drama theater. The former produces only plays in Russian, while the latter specializes in Ukrainian material.

The Ukrainian National Opera in Kiev is famous for its varied repertoire, consisting of both world classics and Ukrainian composers' works. Kharkov, L'viv, and Odesa also have professional opera and ballet companies.

Among the new, experimental theaters, the Kiev theater Koleso (The Wheel) is one of the most notable. The actors of Koleso are young and energetic. Their shows are famous for their interactive nature: actors often invite spectators on stage to take part in the performance. Because of Koleso's popularity, tickets to their performances are sought after by theatergoers.

Left: Dancers from one of Ukraine's many professional ballet companies perform a production in Kiev.

Crafts

One Ukrainian craft popular both in Ukraine and among Ukrainian emigrants living abroad is the elaborately painted Easter egg, *pysanka* (PEA-sahn-kah).

The Ukrainian painted egg is decorated using wax and colored dyes. A pattern is drawn on the egg in wax. Then the egg is dipped in dye. Where there is wax on the egg, the dye's color will not appear. After the dyeing process is complete, the wax is melted off. Real eggshells are used, but occasionally souvenir eggs are made of painted wood.

A pysanka can feature many specific designs, each of them possessing a special meaning. For example, some people believe a ladder symbolizes prosperity or a prayer, while a diamond means knowledge, and poppies represent joy and beauty.

Traditionally, every pysanka was supposed to carry a deep religious meaning. For Ukrainian emigrants, the painted egg is a strong link to their native land and Ukraine's struggle for freedom and independence.

Above: **The brightly colored pysanka has religious and traditional meanings for Ukrainian people.**

Leisure and Festivals

Social Interaction

Guests invited to a Ukrainian household should be prepared for a big meal. Relatives may even come from other towns and villages to greet a special guest. On special occasions, such as birthdays or weddings, Ukrainians have a lengthy festive gathering, with lots of food, drink, toasts, and even singing and dancing. Ukrainians consider interacting with family and friends very important.

WEDDINGS: UKRAINIAN STYLE

A traditional Ukrainian village wedding is a complex affair that involves certain rituals and traditions.
(A Closer Look, page 72)

In Ukraine, several generations of the same family often live close to one another or even in the same household. Grown-up children usually take care of elderly parents, while grandparents are often willing to help raise grandchildren.

Young people, especially in cities, like to spend their leisure time with friends in cafés and bars. Most large cities and many towns have parks where people gather on weekends. Parks often attract chess and soccer players, who play and discuss their favorite games.

Above: Ukrainians are very social people and regard contact between family and friends as an important part of their lives.

Vacations

Most Ukrainians prefer July or August holidays, although winter skiing vacations at home and overseas have become popular in recent years. Crimea, in the southern part of the country, is still the most popular summer destination. Since foreign travel is no longer restricted, as it was under Soviet rule, more overseas destinations are available to Ukrainian travelers. Among foreign summer destinations, the most popular is nearby Turkey. Travel to nearby eastern Europe and the Russian Federation are also popular with Ukrainians.

The majority of Ukrainians take one vacation per year, usually ranging from ten to as many as twenty days. Ukraine also has several public holidays during the year, allowing most people to take additional time off work.

Those who cannot afford to travel far for a vacation either spend free time at home with their families or go to the beach or on a fishing trip for the day. Many Ukrainians own small plots of land and summerhouses outside the cities, and these places are popular with vacationers from urban areas.

Above: **The seaside attractions of Yalta and the Crimean Peninsula make the region a popular holiday and tourist destination.**

News and Entertainment

Television is the main source of news for Ukrainians. Most regions of the country have access to several television stations. Cable television is only starting to become popular in big cities. In addition to Ukrainian stations, Russian television can be watched in eastern Ukraine, while Polish, Hungarian, and Slovak broadcasts are widely available in the west. Western, particularly American, movies, soap operas, and sports programs are the most popular shows.

Until about 1991, Ukrainians subscribed to numerous newspapers and magazines. An average family could receive up to five different daily newspapers, plus one or two weeklies. After the collapse of the united Soviet newspaper and media market in the early 1990s, the print media took some time to regain popularity. Now, every region of Ukraine has numerous newspapers and magazines covering a variety of topics and reflecting different political and ideological positions.

Each large city has about a dozen radio stations, which broadcast news, talk programs, and a wide range of music.

Above: Customers flock to a newspaper stand. Most regions of Ukraine have several different newspapers and magazines to choose from.

Sports

The most popular sport among Ukrainians of all ages is soccer. Games in the Ukrainian Premier League are attended by tens of thousands of fans every weekend. Ukrainian soccer fans also follow the careers of their countrymen who play the game abroad. The most famous of these players currently is the AC Milan striker Andriy Shevchenko, who in the 1999–2000 season became the top scorer in the Italian Serie A league.

Other popular sports in Ukraine are track and field events and gymnastics. Pole-vaulter Sergey Bubka of Donets'k won six world championships and one Olympic title. He also broke the world record many times. Ukrainian gymnasts have won numerous medals and various international competitions.

At the 2000 Olympic Games in Sydney, Yana Klochkova won two gold medals in swimming, and Mykola Milchev won a gold for skeet shooting.

GYMNASTIC SUCCESS STORY

Since independence, Ukraine's gymnasts have won numerous competitions at European, world, and Olympic levels. Budding champions start young in the pursuit of success.
(*A Closer Look, page 48*)

Below: Ukraine's Andriy Shevchenko (*center*) evades a tackle during an international soccer game against England at Wembley in May 2000.

Christmas Celebrations

Eastern Orthodox Christmas falls on January 7, instead of December 25, because of the Orthodox Church's historical use of a different calendar system, which differs in length from the more commonly used Julian calendar. During the Soviet era, the authorities did not encourage Christmas celebrations because the holiday was a religious one. As a result, the New Year became the main winter holiday for the majority of people in Ukraine.

As more and more Ukrainians embrace religion and attend church, Christmas is gaining popularity. Large, colorful Christmas services are held in churches and cathedrals all over the country. Ukraine's president and members of the government have attended the Christmas service in Kiev's main cathedral, the Volodymyr Cathedral, for several years.

On Christmas Eve, children go from house to house singing special songs called *kolyadky* (koh-LJAHD-kee). These songs are similar to Christmas carols. After the children sing, the inhabitants of the house give the children candy or small amounts of money for their performances.

Below: **On Christmas Eve, young Ukrainians visit neighbors' houses to perform kolyadky, which are similar to Christmas carols.**

New Year Festivities

New Year's Eve celebrations are a big occasion for the majority of Ukrainians. Ukrainians usually make special festive dishes and drinks and invite friends to parties. In the country's major cities, New Year's Eve celebrations are large-scale events, with street festivals, fireworks, and parties that last through the night. Although some Ukrainians may prefer a quieter celebration, very few people do not mark the arrival of January 1.

Malanka is a Ukrainian folk holiday. It falls on January 13, according to the Julian calendar, but it is celebrated as New Year's Eve in the old Eastern Orthodox calendar system. Malanka commemorates the feast day of Saint Melania. On this night in Ukraine, carolers traditionally go from house to house playing pranks or acting out a small play. Malanka is usually the final highlight of the Christmas holiday season and is often the last opportunity for partying before the solemn period of Lent, a time of prayer before Easter, begins.

Above: Flowers are an important part of several Ukrainian celebrations, including Easter, spring, and harvest festivals.

IVANA KUPALA: NATURE'S FESTIVAL

The festival of the Night of Ivana Kupala is a midsummer celebration of love, fertility, and folk art. Popular in the western part of rural Ukraine, the festival dates back to pagan times when nature was thought to have special, magical powers.

(*A Closer Look*, page 50)

Food

Ukrainians enjoy good food and go to great lengths and expense to prepare special meals for family, friends, and themselves. Ukrainian food includes everyday dishes and festive dishes, both simple and elaborate. Some dishes are quick and easy to cook, while others take almost all day to prepare. The most common dishes are enjoyed everywhere — what is popular in one area of Ukraine is likely to be popular in another.

Historically, Ukraine has been an agricultural country, and the favorite dishes of the nation reflect this farming influence. Ukrainians use a lot of grain and other locally grown foods in their cooking. Potatoes and potato dishes are popular, as is bread.

During summer, most people eat a lot of fresh fruits and vegetables. Many Ukrainian families make their own fruit and vegetable preserves for winter, when fresh fruits and vegetables become too expensive to buy.

Meats Ukrainians typically eat are beef, pork, and chicken. Fish is not popular but is available in most restaurants and makes an occasional appearance on the family dining table.

Above: **Bread is a staple part of the Ukrainian diet and makes use of the country's large grain resources.**

Favorite Dishes

Borsch (BOHRSH), a soup made with cabbage, beets, and tomatoes, is, without a doubt, Ukrainians' favorite first course with a main meal. When made with beef, borsch is served hot; otherwise the soup is eaten cold. Some people like the soup with sour cream or with different types of garlic bread. *Holubtsi* (hohloob-TSI), or ground beef and rice wrapped in cabbage leaves and usually served with a thick gravy, is also among Ukrainians' favorite dishes.

The main course in a Ukrainian meal is usually a combination of meat or fish, potatoes, hot cereal, or noodles. In summer, fresh fruits and vegetables are also served, while in winter homemade preserves, such as pickled cucumbers, sweet peppers, or tomatoes, accompany dishes.

VARENYKY: THE NATIONAL DISH

Varenyky (vah-REH-nee-kee) are semicircular dumplings that can be filled with just about anything, ranging from meat to fruit. The more popular fillings include potatoes, cabbage, cottage cheese, and strawberries. Varenyky are enjoyed by Ukrainians as both an everyday and a festive dish.

(A Closer Look, page 68)

Above: This typical Ukrainian table is laid with the favorite first course of borsch.

Ukrainian desserts usually contain fried or baked dough. Various kinds of pies and cakes are also popular. Most Ukrainians end the meal with a drink of tea or coffee or a fruit compote.

Ukrainians' main meal is usually in the evening when the entire family returns home from work or school. On weekends, when the family is at home, the main meal shifts to the middle of the day.

A CLOSER LOOK AT UKRAINE

A quest for true independence dominates Ukrainian life. For centuries, the people inhabiting the territory of Ukraine fought to escape the rule of neighboring nations. Only since independence in 1991 has the country been free from control by another nation.

From the tales of the legendary Kozaks to the political activities of the current younger generation, independence is a familiar thread running through Ukrainian life and culture, especially in the poems of Ukrainian's most famous literary poet Taras Shevchenko.

Opposite: **Winter snows cling to buildings and trees in the Carpathian region of Ukraine.**

Now free to express its culture without repression, Ukraine is full of traditional festivals and entertainment, as the Ukrainian people pass on to future generations what the country's repressive rulers prohibited in the past.

Life in Ukraine, however, is not without its problems. The sudden change from Soviet rule brought about harsh economic adjustments, and the 1986 Chernobyl nuclear accident still affects Ukraine's people and environment today.

Above: **Farmers harvest their crops from the rich soils of the Ukrainian steppe.**

Chernobyl's Nuclear Catastrophe

The name Chernobyl will forever be associated with the worst nuclear disaster in the history of humankind. At approximately 1:23 a.m. on April 26, 1986, reactor unit 4 at the Chernobyl (also known as Chornobyl) nuclear power plant near Kiev exploded. The blast occurred during a safety procedure experiment, and it released a massive amount of radioactive material into the air. The material was carried by the wind and spread over Belarus, Russia, and Ukraine, and as far west as France and Italy.

Fatal Exposure

Two power plant workers were killed in the Chernobyl reactor explosion. More explosions started a fire and blew off the lid of the reactor. The firefighters who put out the fire paid for their success with their lives. More than thirty firefighters died afterward from radiation exposure. In addition, the 30,000 inhabitants of the town of Pripyat, where many of the power plant workers lived, were evacuated. All the residents had to leave their homes, their belongings, and their whole lives behind.

Below: Engineers inspect the damage caused by the explosion at the Chernobyl nuclear power plant three days after the accident.

Left: **An elderly woman visits the grave of a Chernobyl victim. The effects of the accident are still felt today. The nuclear fallout from the accident was many times worse than the radiation from the atomic bombs dropped on Japan's Hiroshima and Nagasaki at the end of World War II.**

Lasting Effects

The Chernobyl disaster affected Ukraine in a number of ways. At the time, the exposure to radiation was expected to affect the health of tens of thousands of people through illnesses such as cancer. Other effects included a decrease in birthrates, a shortage of labor around Kiev from the migration of people to other areas of the country, and the slowdown of agricultural and industrial production due to radiation contamination.

In December 2000, the Ukrainian government, under pressure from the European Union and other international organizations, shut down the last working reactor at Chernobyl. The problem of Chernobyl, however, is not solved with the closure of the plant. The damaged reactor was housed in a concrete sarcophagus designed to stop radiation leaks, but this structure has weakened, and urgent repairs are required to contain its dangerous contents.

Dances of the Soul

The music is slow and quiet at first, and the dancers' motions are smooth. The performers seem to be just walking around the stage to the rhythm of the music, not dancing. Seconds later, the melody speeds up a little and becomes louder. The dancers respond with faster motions and more energetic gestures. The music then becomes even faster and louder; the dancers accelerate, as if competing with the sounds. A minute into the dance, the song

is loud and furiously fast. The dancers, men in the foreground and women in back, have no trouble keeping pace. The men, often dressed in white, red, and black embroidered shirts, bright-red loose pants called *sharovary* (shah-roh-VAH-reeh), and red or black boots, move toward the front of the stage and perform leaps and turns worthy of Olympic athletes. The women stay in the background at first, as if providing a backdrop to the men's furious motions, but then they also move forward and join the men in this fast dance. This dance is *hopak* (hoh-PAHK) — one of the best-known and most unique of the Ukrainian folk dances.

Above: **Ukrainian folk dancers are known for their colorful costumes.**

Legends Expressed in Dance

Ukrainian folk dances use songs and ballads to portray the country's history and legends. Through the dances, Ukrainians express their hopes, customs, and traditions. Some of the dances are fast and athletic, such as the hopak; others are slow and solemn. Some popular themes include love and family, the change of seasons, harvests, and other farming activities.

Dancers, through their movements and gestures, also portray events that occur in everyday life. Through skillful moves, a people's way of life or a trade or occupation can be displayed

through dance. Based on traditional folk culture, Ukrainian dances vary by region in choreographic method, content, dynamics, costumes, and musical accompaniment. Ukrainian dancing has roots in ancient times, when the dances were considered a ritual of communicating with the forces of nature.

Folk dancing is one of Ukraine's more visible exports to other countries. Many Ukrainian immigrants and descendents form their own dance groups and schools in their new countries, and Ukrainian professional dancing companies travel the world performing to audiences.

Above: **Ukrainian children are taught their country's traditional dances at a young age.**

Gymnastic Success Story

The 2000 Olympic Games in Sydney, Australia, showed once again that Ukraine is a world gymnastics power. The Ukrainian men's team won the silver medal in the artistic team competition, and Olexsandr Beresh took the bronze in the men's individual all-around event. The Ukrainian women's team placed high in the artistic and trampoline events.

The performance at Sydney was neither the first nor the most successful showing for Ukrainian gymnasts. In addition to Olympic medals, Ukrainian gymnasts have won several prizes at top World and European competitions. After winning a gold medal at the 1996 Atlanta Olympic Games, Lilia Podkopayeva held the Olympic, World, and European all-around titles at the same time.

As part of the Soviet Union, Ukraine benefited from the expertise of the Soviets in the field of gymnastics, and today Ukrainian gymnasts continue to use the knowledge and experience of famous Soviet coaches and athletes. Ukraine's gymnastics program is supported mainly by the government, so recent economic problems and a lack of money make it difficult for Ukraine to build new facilities. Nevertheless, the gymnasts still manage to achieve international success due to their commitment to the sport and determination to succeed.

In recent decades, the sport of gymnastics has become the domain of the very young, especially in women's competition. Seventeen-, sixteen-, and even fifteen-year-old athletes compete in the world's premier competitions. Unfortunately, the career of a professional gymnast is also short. Lilia Podkopayeva retired when she was only twenty.

The most famous gymnastics training facility in Ukraine is the National Training Center, in the town of Koncha-Zaspa, near Kiev. Built more than twenty-five years ago as a local training facility, the base is the center of the Ukrainian gymnastics program — the Ukrainian men's and women's teams train here. Both teams have nicknames: the women's team is called the Ultra Ukes, while the men's is known as the Tryzub Titans.

STARTING YOUNG

Children with the talent to become good gymnasts, such as this young girl (*above*), start training at a young age. Professional gymnastic scouts visit physical education lessons in elementary schools to find future stars. When the scouts find potential champions, they contact the parents and encourage them to let their children pursue gymnastics. These children continue to live at home and go to school. Every day after school, however, they train hard for success.

Opposite: Ukraine's Olena Vitrychenko performs a routine during the individual rhythmic gymnastic final at the Sydney 2000 Olympic Games.

Ivana Kupala: Nature's Festival

On July 7, when the Ukrainian summer is normally warm and free of bad weather, many people across the country take part in the celebration of the Night of Ivana Kupala. This festival, celebrated widely in the rural areas of western Ukraine, dates back to pre-Christian times, when people worshiped many different gods and believed nature had a special magical power that was capable of changing their lives for the better.

Left: **The Night of Ivana Kupala is similar to other harvest festivals celebrated in Ukraine's rural western regions.**

Left: **The Night of Ivana Kupala has special significance for young women, who perform rituals to find out about their marriage prospects.**

During the Night of Ivana Kupala, many plants and herbs are believed to acquire healing powers. According to old myths about the festival, the night of July 7 also is the only time of the year when ferns blossom, and whoever finds fern flowers in the forest in the middle of this night will be happy, lucky, and wealthy. Anyone wanting to find the blossoms must know that only nine-year-old ferns can bloom. Those gathering the flowers spread a silk kerchief under the fern's fronds for the blossom to fall on to.

Marriage Predictions

During the Night of Ivana Kupala, young unmarried women sing special songs about love and marriage. At dawn, they go to a riverbank and set fresh flowers afloat in the river. If the river takes a woman's flowers downstream, the woman will soon be happily married. If the river returns the flowers, the woman has to wait at least another year for a groom. People also perform other rituals to ensure the fertility of the fields and a good harvest in autumn.

With the coming of Christianity to Ukraine, churches tried to suppress the holiday, which they considered a pagan celebration. Unable to stop people from celebrating this festival, Christian leaders combined Ivana Kupala with the Christian feast day of John the Baptist.

Kiev: Cradle of Ukrainian Civilization

Ukraine's capital city of Kiev preserves much of its historic heritage while reinventing and revitalizing itself according to changing times. Early settlements in the area date back tens of thousands of years, but today's Kiev was probably founded more than fifteen hundred years ago.

Legendary Origins

A popular Ukrainian legend about Kiev's origins tells the story of three brothers who each established a settlement in the area. These settlements became the town of Kiev, named after the eldest brother, Kiy. This account is very popular among Ukrainians — when the city celebrated its fifteen-hundred-year anniversary in the 1980s, statues of the three brothers and their sister, Lybid, were erected on one of the embankments along the Dnipro River.

The city grew in prominence between the ninth and thirteenth centuries as the center of the ancient civilization of the Kievan Rus kingdom, with its magnificent churches and other

Left: **The impressive Saint Sophia Cathedral, with its many domes, is a major landmark in Kiev.**

impressive buildings. Medieval Kiev was known throughout Europe for its beauty and vitality and for its architectural, artistic, musical, language, and literary contributions.

Above: **The newly named Independence Square, formerly known as October Revolution Square, is situated near the main Kiev thoroughfare of Khreshchatyk Avenue.**

Historical Highlights

Since Ukrainian independence, Kiev has received massive financial investment from the West, allowing the city to create new jobs, build new facilities, and improve its standard of living. Despite the renovations, downtown Kiev is still soaked in history and tradition. The main chestnut tree-lined Khreshchatyk Avenue leads to Vladimir Hill, named after the ruler of the Ukrainian state of Kievan Rus — Saint Vladimir.

Farther up the hill is a street named Andriyivsky Uzviz, or Andrew's Descent. This twisting road winds its way through lush hills looking over the Dnipro River. On the street is the small Andriyivska Church, which was designed in 1754 by the Russian Imperial Court's Italian-born architect Bartolomeo Rastrelli.

Two other famous historic landmarks in Kiev are the Saint Sophia Cathedral and the Kyevo-Pecherska Lavra, or Monastery of the Caves. Saint Sophia's distinct domes can be seen from anywhere in central Kiev, and the monastery is famous for its underground passages and its collection of religious exhibits.

Kozaks: Warrior Race

The Ukrainian Kozaks, or Cossacks, are best known as fierce warriors. Their main camps were close to the modern city of Zaporizhzhya, along the banks of the Dnipro River, halfway between Kiev and the southern steppe. The Kozaks are usually remembered as strong men with shaved heads and long mustaches. The trademark of the Kozaks' intimidating appearance is a long and narrow clump of hair that hangs down, and to the side, from an otherwise hairless scalp. This clump of hair is called *oseledets* (oh-seh-LEH-dehts). Kozaks also often fought without shirts, which gave them an even more intimidating and savage appearance.

Military Mercenaries

After the fifteenth century, the word *Kozak* described peasants who fled serfdom in Poland, Lithuania, and the Moscow-centered principality of Muscovy to start self-governing military communities in the Dnipro region. These Kozaks evolved into a military force, sometimes fighting for freedom and sometimes for money as mercenaries. They were allies to many people and

Below: **A modern-day version of a Kozak shows his intimidating appearance, including a long mustache and shaved head.**

states, including the Ukrainian princes under Polish occupation and the Russian Empire. As Kozak armies grew larger, they built fortresses along the Dnipro. A Kozak fortress is called a *sich* (SEECH). The word *sich* in Ukrainian roughly means "a fortress built from trees." Everything in a sich, including the tall fence around it, was built from logs.

Legends of the Kozaks

The Kozaks' bravery is commemorated in Ukrainian folklore. The traveling minstrels, the kobzari, sang songs about a brave Kozak showing up at a critical moment to save a poor peasant or a beautiful woman from Turkish oppression. One famous image of Kozaks appears in the Ilya Repin painting *Zaporozhian Cossacks* about the Kozaks' conflict against the Turks.

Mykola Lysenko: Musical Founder

Considered by many to be the founder of Ukrainian classical music, composer Mykola Vitaliyovych Lysenko (1842–1912) is the author of eleven operas — eight of which are based on Ukrainian stories and themes — and numerous choral and piano pieces, as well as works for Ukraine's national instrument, the bandura. His other achievements include putting to music more than one hundred poems by the great Ukrainian poet Taras Shevchenko. Lysenko is also credited with encouraging Ukrainian music education by founding a musical institute in Kiev in 1904.

Lysenko is best known for his operas. His important operas, which brought him recognition both at home and abroad, include the comedy *Natalka Poltavka* (1889) and the historic work *Taras Bulba* (1890), based on the novella by Nikolai Gogol (1809–1852). *Taras Bulba*, a large-scale work, could not be produced in Ukraine because of a lack of resources to stage it. The opera did not see its premiere until 1924 — twelve years after the composer died.

Above: **Mykola Lysenko's contribution to Ukrainian music and culture is marked in Kiev with a monument to the composer.**

Toils of a Lifetime

Throughout his life and career, Lysenko felt that promoting Ukrainian national music and culture was his major mission. When creating his music, he tried to use Ukrainian themes, characters, and musical heritage. He saw music not only as a beautiful and fulfilling form of art but also as a way to awaken people's national and cultural conscience by putting them in touch with their culture and history.

Lysenko was born in a small village in the region around Poltava. His mother taught him to play the piano when he was a child. In 1860, he studied music at Kharkov, and in 1864 he finished his university studies in Kiev. From 1867 to 1869 he continued his piano studies in Leipzig, Germany, and returned to Kiev to teach piano in 1869. Lysenko worked hard to promote

Ukrainian music on his return to Kiev. He gave piano concerts, organized choirs, and toured throughout the country. As a music ethnographer, he traveled throughout the countryside, collecting and recording songs and melodies.

In the 1990s, Ukraine recognized Lysenko's contribution to the nation's culture by issuing several postage stamps commemorating the composer.

Above: **A young Ukrainian violinist plays a tune. Mykola Lysenko is credited with fostering Ukrainian music education.**

The Politics of Youth

Young Ukrainians have forced the government to change its policies twice in recent years, by organizing mass demonstrations, in which students, young workers, and young intellectuals took to the streets to protest.

When economic reforms started in Ukraine in the early 1990s, they hit young people hard. Education, previously free, suddenly became expensive. The unemployment rate among young people also jumped to about 30 percent by 1998 after plants and factories cut jobs to become more efficient. Harsh economic realities prompted many young Ukrainians to become politically active.

Youthful Pressure

In October 1990, Kiev students began a campaign of peaceful protests to speed up political reforms designed to increase Ukraine's independence from the Soviet Union. They used a variety of nonviolent tactics, including a hunger strike in the city's main square, school boycotts, protests, and occupation

Below: **Student hunger strikers camped in the streets of downtown Kiev during their 1990 demonstration. They wanted to force the government to speed up Ukraine's split from the Soviet Union.**

of government buildings. The students gradually escalated the conflict, forcing the government to respond either with massive repression or major concessions. Fifteen days after the protests started, the government gave in to the students' demands and Ukraine's parliament was forced to adopt new laws. The students had won the battle.

Above: **Protests have been a familiar sight during Ukraine's short history of democracy.**

Continuing Protests

In the summer of 2000, Ukrainian students rose again to protest against the government's economic policies. This time, the demonstrations were less intense than in 1990, and they consisted of several peaceful marches on parliament and government buildings. The demonstrators demanded the resignation of President Leonid Kuchma (1938–) who, they believed, was not doing enough to improve the nation's economy. Kuchma kept his job, but parliament again passed new laws to satisfy some of the protesters' demands. One of the organizers of this protest and the protest in 1990 was the Union of Ukrainian Students — one of the most powerful youth organizations in the country.

Pottery From the Past

Two internationally known styles of ceramics have their origins in Ukraine — Opishnya and Hutsul. The two styles are artistically different and come from different parts of the country. Opishnya pottery comes from central Ukraine, while Hutsul ceramics hail from the Carpathian Mountains in the western part of the country.

Center of Ceramics

About 30 miles (48 km) from Poltava is the small village of Opishnya. The village is Ukraine's oldest and most famous ceramics center. Opishnya ceramics are often strange and

Left: **An Opishnya potter adds the finishing touches to his ceramic creation.**

Left: **Opishnya artists draw inspiration from the region's rich heritage of folk tales and legends to produce unusual ceramic creations, including mythical animals.**

intriguing. Along with the usual round, square, and oval pots and bowls that can be used in the kitchen, Opishnya ceramic artists use their nation's heritage of folk tales, legends, and mysterious characters to create one of the world's more unusual collections of ceramic figures.

One of the favored themes in Opishnya pottery is animals. Elaborate horses, bulls, and sheep are the village artists' trademark. Among the most popular Opishnya artifacts are horse- and bull-shaped water jugs, sheep-shaped storage containers for rice and flour, and pig-shaped pots for candy.

Opishnya has a large museum that houses an impressive collection of pottery. Its pots are also sold at fairs and festivals.

Product of the Highlands

Hutsul ceramics are named after the Hutsul people — the highlanders of the Carpathian Mountains in western Ukraine. The Hutsuls have a reputation as skilled craftspeople, known for their wood carving, brass work, and rug weaving, as well as their famous pottery. While Opishnya ceramics often portray legendary creatures, the Hutsul pottery is more down-to-earth and usually pictures geometric designs, scenes from everyday life, and some religious themes. Hutsul pottery is characterized by clear-cut, geometric drawings. The color scheme of Hutsul ceramics usually includes green, yellow, red, and black.

Taras Shevchenko: Literary Legend

Ukraine's greatest and best-known literary figure is poet and painter Taras Shevchenko (1814–1861). As a son of poor farmers, the young Shevchenko was virtually the slave of a wealthy family. Artists who knew the family, however, noticed his talent and helped buy Shevchenko's freedom. He was then able to study at the St. Petersburg Academy of the Arts with the Russian painter Karl Bryullov (1799–1852). After completing his studies at the Russian academy, Shevchenko continued to paint, but it was his poetry that brought him international fame.

Early Works

Shevchenko's most famous early work is the collection of poetry *Kobzar* (*The Minstrel*, 1840). Most poems in this romantic collection remember Ukraine's heroic and epic past and describe the Kozaks and their wars with foreign invaders.

Later, the topics and tone of Shevchenko's poetry changed. To his usual romanticism, he added open opposition to the Russian imperial authorities. His poems became militant, calling for disobedience and foretelling a revolution. The epic poem

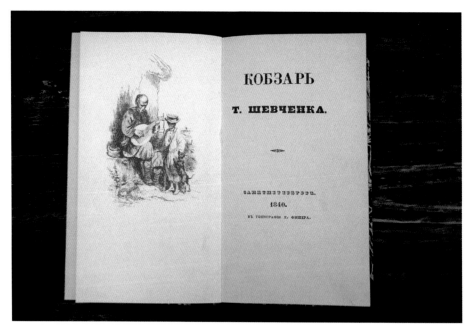

Left: Dealing with Ukraine's heroic and epic history, *Kobzar* is a collection of Taras Shevchenko's early poetic works.

Left: **Taras Shevchenko is revered by Ukrainians everywhere for his efforts to promote independence through his poetry.**

Haidamaky ("The Haidamaks," 1841) combined Ukrainian romanticism and legends, with calls to end Russian political and cultural oppression. The poem is an allegory, or symbolic representation, of Ukraine's struggle for freedom. The Russians, wanting to stop Shevchenko from writing, sentenced him to exile and compulsory military service in 1847.

Ukrainian Exile

Banned from writing or painting while in the army, the poet kept a secret diary, where he wrote drafts of new poems and sketched new pictures. This diary became famous after his death. An edition of it, with reproductions of all the poet's handwriting and drawings, was made more than a century after he died.

To Ukrainians all over the world, the name of Taras Shevchenko is a spiritual and intellectual symbol of Ukraine. His poems and biographies have been translated into dozens of languages and are widely available and recognized in the West.

Sorochintsy's Fairground Attractions

Sorochintsy, a small town about 60 miles (96 km) from Poltava, comes alive during the last weekend of August, as colorful and interesting characters from Ukraine's past invade its sleepy streets and markets. The Sorochintsy Fair is one of the oldest and most exciting events in Ukraine's cultural and commercial life. The event attracts tens of thousands of visitors from all over the country, Europe, and abroad.

Something for Everyone

The fair is held over three days on a large square outside the town. Merchants flock to Sorochintsy hoping to sell their goods at a profitable price, while tourists come looking for a bargain. The fair has it all: food, drinks, clothes, housewares, and even cattle and pets.

Besides being a trading place, the fair is also a large outdoor theater. In the spirit of old-time summer fairs that combined trade with entertainment, fair organizers erect stages all over the

Left: **A wide variety of food and drink tempt many visitors to the Sorochintsy Fair.**

fairgrounds. Actors wearing Ukrainian folk costumes or dressed up as various strange and mysterious creatures act out comedies, legends, and fairy tales on stage and among the crowd.

Above: **Animal and agricultural exhibitions feature prominently at the Sorochintsy Fair.**

Literary Tribute

Much of the theatrical action at the fair centers on the literary heritage of the nineteenth century writer Nikolai Gogol, who was born near Sorochintsy. Gogol's writing is full of mythical characters, such as mermaids, forest creatures, and talking animals. His stories are also tributes to the resourceful and humorous Ukrainian villager. Excerpts from these stories are among the most popular dramas staged at Sorochintsy.

The performances at Sorochintsy try to capture both the supernatural and the everyday aspects of Gogol's work. A highlight of the fair is an actor impersonating the author, who quietly walks around as if watching performances of his own works and evaluating them. Photographs taken with the Gogol impersonator are always popular with visitors to the fair.

The Ukrainian Riviera

Ukraine's premier resort area, the Crimean Peninsula is a popular summer vacation destination for many people in Ukraine, Russia, and other neighboring countries. Located on the Black Sea in southern Ukraine, Crimea has all the necessary ingredients for a vacation: deep blue sea, sunny beaches, hiking, and plenty of historic and cultural monuments. The Crimean Mountains cross the peninsula in the south, making the region popular among rock climbers.

City by the Sea

One of the most interesting places in Crimea is Yalta, a city located on the southern coast of the peninsula. As it approaches the sea, the main road to Yalta from inland first winds among the yellow and brown Crimean Mountains, offering views of grapes growing on the mountainsides. Then the road takes a sharp turn, and Yalta is nestled in the valley below, between the mountains and the sea.

The city buildings are predominantly white and light gray and are separated by green patches of parks and tree-lined streets. Shielded from the rest of the peninsula by the mountains, Yalta

Below: **With its fairy-tale architecture, the Swallow's Nest castle is a prominent landmark on the Crimean Peninsula.**

Above: **Built as a summer home for the Russian czar between 1910 and 1911, Yalta's Livadiya Palace has a museum, gallery, and extensive gardens.**

enjoys a special climate of its own. The weather may be cloudy and rainy a short distance away beyond the mountains, while it is sunny and hot in the city. The Mediterranean-type climate makes the city, and its surroundings, an excellent place for holidays and agriculture. The place to be for Yalta nightlife is the Embankment, where hotels, restaurants, bars, and clubs face out toward the sea.

Historic Homes

Probably the most famous person who lived in Yalta was the renowned Russian writer Anton Chekhov (1860–1904). Chekhov and his family moved to Yalta in 1899 because the Crimean climate was good for the writer's ailing health. Chekhov lived in Yalta on and off until his death. Chekhov's house is now home to a museum that honors his life and work.

A short boat ride from Yalta is Livadiya, the marble summer residence of the last Russian czar Nicholas II (1868-1918). In 1945, the palace hosted the famous Yalta Conference, during which the governments of the United States, Soviet Union, and Great Britain agreed on the future of post-World War II Europe. The palace is now a museum.

Varenyky: The National Dish

While Italy is often associated with pasta, France with wine and cheese, and America with hamburgers, Ukraine is linked to varenyky. Over time, varenyky have become more than food to Ukrainians. They are the subject of folk tales, songs, and poems. Varenyky are so well known and made so often that some Ukrainian cookbooks use the phrase "make the dough as for varenyky" in recipes; no further explanation is needed.

Simple but Satisfying

Varenyky are dough dumplings with a filling. The type of filling is open to the imagination. Anything can be used for fillings, ranging from meat and fish to vegetables, such as cabbage or potatoes, and even strawberries and cherries. More creative cooks are known to put plums and apricots inside varenyky. These dumplings can be either savory and sweet and served as a main dish, an appetizer, or a dessert.

Below: **A simple dish to make, varenyky need only dough and the imagination to create its fillings.**

Left: Once the focal point of celebratory meals, varenyky is now an everyday dish in Ukraine.

Varenyky's origins are linked to the days when Ukrainian cuisine consisted of only a few kinds of meat, vegetables, and fruit. With this small number of ingredients, varenyky took center stage, since they can have a wide variety of fillings. They may have started as a festive dish, but they are now a popular everyday food.

Varenyky promote culinary individuality: some cooks prefer thick, heavy varenyky, while others like light and delicate ones. A potato and cheese filling is one of the plumpest, and the dough is made thicker for this filling than for sauerkraut or cabbage fillings. Fruit-filled varenyky are made with lighter dough. The recipe omits eggs, making the dough somewhat similar to that used for pizza — tough and simple.

More Than Just Food

Making varenyky is fun and often involves the whole family. Children help make the dough, cut out circles, and add fillings.

Varenyky are part of Ukrainian folklore and even literature. Songs, poems, and jokes have been written about them. One of Nikolai Gogol's humorous stories about life in a Ukrainian village highlights the popularity of this dish among Ukrainians. In the story, a character wastes his magic powers eating varenyky "hands-free," by commanding them to jump from the plate, take a dip in a bowl of sour cream, and jump into his mouth.

Village Life

The Ukrainian village is not simply a place on a map
or a collection of streets, houses, and people's addresses; it is
a place of ethnic, cultural, and spiritual heritage. Life is slow,
simple, and somewhat old fashioned. Many Ukrainian villages
look and feel as if they are frozen in time, not because they lack
the facilities of the big cities, but because they treasure and
preserve the old values, habits, and Ukrainian way of life.

Community Spirit

Friendship and camaraderie exist among villagers. Together they
harvest crops, celebrate births, and mourn deaths. Most villagers
know one another and greet one another in the streets. Even
when they meet strangers, villagers greet them, strike up
a conversation, and make them feel welcome.

Left: **Villagers in the Ukrainian countryside often cling to ways of the past.**

Every family in a Ukrainian village tries to be economically self-sufficient. Around every house, sizeable plots of land are farmed for fruits and vegetables. The plot where vegetables are grown is called *ogorod* (oh-goh-ROHD), and the fruit section is called *sad* (SAHD). The average Ukrainian village family works hard on its plot of land. When the fruits and vegetables are harvested, most are for the family, while the surplus is often sold at the local market.

Above: **Villagers work hard on their plots of land, growing enough fruits and vegetables to be self-sufficient.**

Surviving Tough Times

When Ukraine embarked on radical economic reforms in the early 1990s, many young people moved to large cities to get a college education or a better paying job. Consequently, some villages began to be described as "dying" because they were populated mostly by the elderly. Some rural areas, however, started experiencing population growth after Ukraine's independence. As the rapid change to a free-market economy forced many city dwellers into poverty, a number of these people moved to villages to try and make a living off the land.

Weddings: Ukrainian Style

The traditional Ukrainian wedding is a complex affair with many rituals. Traditional ceremonies are more common in the countryside; people getting married in the city usually prefer a simpler, modern ceremony.

Elaborate Traditions

The traditional village wedding usually starts with a formal engagement. The groom and several respected elders — usually older, married men called *starosty* (STAH-rohs-tee) — visit the home of the bride to make a marriage request to her parents and exchange gifts. The groom's party brings a bottle of Ukrainian vodka called *horilka* (hoh-REEL-kah), and the bride drapes the elders with a ritual embroidered towel, or *rushnyk* (roosh-NIHK). Both parties provide a traditional loaf of bread for one another.

Below: **A wedding engagement requires village elders called starosty to visit the bride's home. Traditional loaves of bread are used to make the marriage request.**

The traditional Ukrainian engagement can be as short as one week — the time needed to cook and prepare for the wedding celebration. The ritual part of the marriage process begins on the Thursday or Friday before the actual wedding with the baking of a special elaborate bread called *korovai* (koh-roh-VAHJ).

Above: **A Ukrainian wedding uses a number of rituals during the ceremony, often to symbolize the couple's unity.**

Let the Party Begin

On Friday night and Saturday morning, the bride and groom walk around the village inviting their respective wedding guests. Friday evening is usually reserved for *devich vechir* (DEH-vich VEH-cheer), a party where the bride bids farewell to her unmarried female friends.

On Saturday, a civil marriage contract is signed. The church ceremony, if there is one, takes place on Sunday. During the ceremony, the couple must stand on the rushnyk, which symbolizes their unity. After the ceremony, the towel is given to the groom's mother, who ties the hands of the groom and the bride with it, symbolizing that they are now inseparable.

The ceremonies are usually followed by meals, served at the bride's house first and then at the groom's. Wedding celebrations can last for as long as a week, with the whole village involved.

RELATIONS WITH NORTH AMERICA

Some North Americans may find it difficult to see Ukraine as a sovereign country and not as part of Russia or some other large power. Since the country regained its independence, however, awareness of Ukraine in North America has risen dramatically in the past decade.

Leaders of both the United States and Canada stress the importance of Ukraine in terms of European and global security and peace. Their statements are supported by extensive contacts between the governments of the three countries. Economic, scientific, and cultural exchanges are also increasing.

Opposite: **Brand names such as McDonald's are becoming a more common sight in Ukraine, as the country opens up to investment from North America and other regions.**

The Ukrainian communities in North America work hard to ensure lasting recognition of Ukraine on the continent. North Americans are now visiting Ukraine more than ever before. These foreign visitors come to do business, but they also come to learn about the culture of a country that is reemerging from the shadow of its powerful neighbors.

Many Ukrainian-Americans and Ukrainian-Canadians also go to Ukraine to research their family histories and meet distant relatives for the first time.

Above: **U.S. president Bill Clinton greets enthusiastic Ukrainians on a visit to Kiev in June 2000.**

Left: **In recent years, the United States has been working closely with Ukraine on the continuing problems of nuclear safety, especially at the Chernobyl power plant accident site.**

Relations between Ukraine and North America

When U.S. president Bill Clinton met with his Ukrainian counterpart Leonid Kuchma in Kiev on June 5, 2000, they emphasized the need for both countries to continue strengthening their ties. In the past several years, the United States has declared Ukraine to be one of its foreign policy priorities in Eastern Europe. Ukrainian leaders have stressed the importance of their country's good relations with the United States, understanding the United States' leading role in the world and the benefits of economic cooperation between the countries.

Current areas of cooperation include European security, joint space research, joint economic ventures, and military cooperation. The U.S. government is implementing small-business training programs for Ukrainian businesses to ease their transition into a free-market economy. Scientists from the United States have been working with their Ukrainian colleagues on the problem of Chernobyl and nuclear safety. In the late 1990s, the United States, Canada, and several European countries set up a scientific and technical organization in Ukraine, which is helping steer former military research facilities toward civilian projects. Past areas of cooperation include Ukrainian troops taking part in peacekeeping operations in the former Yugoslavia alongside U.S. soldiers. Cosmonaut Leonid Kadenyuk was the first Ukrainian to travel into space on board a U.S. space shuttle in December 1997.

The exchange of ideas and talent between North America and Ukraine also takes place through the overseas Ukrainian community. Ukrainians, or their descendents, living in North America include scientists, film directors, athletes, and even a former Canadian governor general — Ramon John Hnatyshyn, who served in the post from 1990 to 1995.

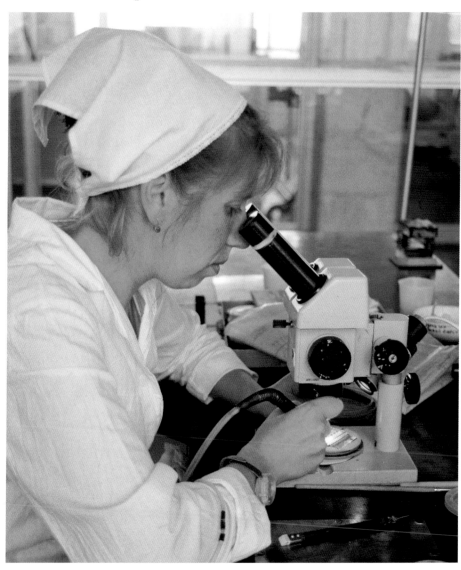

Left: **Scientific research is one area in which Ukraine and North America are forming closer links.**

Early Ukrainian Immigrants to North America

The start of large-scale Ukrainian immigration to the United States began in the late nineteenth century, with most immigrants arriving during the last two decades of the century. Most early immigrants settled in the industrial areas of the country, such as New York, Pennsylvania, and Virginia, because employment, especially in coal mining, was easier to find in these areas.

Many Ukrainians who emigrated to the United States during the first wave were lured by the promise of quick money in North America, even though work there was no less strenuous than the jobs they had left behind in Ukraine. Some Ukrainians who traveled to the United States during this period originally did not want to move permanently. Instead, they wanted to earn enough money to buy a farm in Ukraine and return home to a comfortable life.

When these early immigrants arrived in the United States, however, many realized the promises of the Ukrainian emigration agents were unrealistic. They began to understand that the dishonest agents had swindled them, bringing them to the United

Left: A Ukrainian concert is held at the Ellis Island immigration center in New York at the beginning of the twentieth century. Most of the Ukrainian immigrants coming to the United States passed through the Ellis Island center.

Above: **Ukrainians' experience as farmers was put to good use by the Canadian government, which wanted to develop Canada's western prairies during the nineteenth century.**

States as cheap laborers and as replacement workers for those employees on strike at coal mines and steel mills. Immigrants from other countries were often hostile toward Ukrainians because Ukrainians were so desperate for money they were willing to work under almost any conditions. Often illiterate and unaware of local customs, Ukrainian immigrants did not fear dangerous jobs in the mines and steel mills because they had been toughened by hard labor in their homeland.

The first recorded Ukrainian immigrants to Canada arrived in September 1891. Most nineteenth-century immigrants to Canada came from western Ukraine and were farmers. The Canadian government placed them in new, undeveloped lands in the western part of the country. Without any financial or other assistance from the authorities, Ukrainian farmers were left to develop the prairie wilderness of provinces such as Manitoba, Saskatchewan, and Alberta. By 1903, the first Ukrainian-language newspaper in Canada was printed, closely followed by Ukrainian language books and bookstores to sell them.

Second and Third Waves of Ukrainian Immigration to Canada

The first flow of Ukrainian immigrants to Canada ended with the outbreak of World War I in 1914. Some ten thousand Ukrainians served in the Canadian armed forces during the war, and one, Filip Konowal (1887–1959), won the Victoria Cross for bravery. Ukrainian-Canadians demonstrated a remarkable loyalty to Canada, and many died on the battlefields of Europe.

The second wave of Ukrainian immigration to Canada took place between 1919 and 1939. This wave brought about seventy thousand Ukrainians to Canada, including many Ukrainian political refugees fleeing communist government oppression. With a Ukrainian-Canadian community already in place, they were quickly settled into the new way of life.

After World War II, only a few hundred Ukrainians entered Canada each year, but, with Ukraine's independence in 1991 and the removal of Soviet-imposed travel restrictions, a third wave of immigration to Canada has begun.

Today, about 95 percent of all Canadians who claim Ukrainian ancestry are Canadian-born. Ukrainian-Canadians are no longer an immigrant community, with many now fifth-generation Canadians.

Left: **Canadian troops prepare to board trains for the World War I front lines. Some ten thousand Ukrainian-Canadians fought under the Canadian flag during the war.**

Left: Ukrainian-American William Dzus revolutionized military production with the invention of a screw fastener that did not become loose because of vibration, a vital advancement in the construction of military hardware such as tanks.

Ukrainian-Americans and Ukrainian-Canadians in World War II

Many Ukrainian-Americans and Ukrainian-Canadians served in the armed forces of the United States and Canada during World War II. Over forty thousand served in the Canadian military.

In addition to fighting on the battlefront, Ukrainians in North America contributed to the war effort in many other ways. In 1932, Ukrainian-American William Dzus invented a screw fastener that did not become loose under vibration. The dzus fastener was used on aircraft and military vehicles and was a major contribution to the war effort.

Among the many Ukrainian-American soldiers prominent during World War II was Lieutenant-Colonel Ted Kalakuka from Pennsylvania. The first known Ukrainian-American graduate of West Point Military Academy, Kalakuka was honored for his role in the defense of the Philippines against the Japanese. Kalakuka later died in a prisoner of war camp. Another Ukrainian-American honored in World War II was Nicholas Minue from New Jersey. He was awarded the U.S. Congressional Medal of Honor for his bravery during an attack against a German machine gun post in Tunisia, North Africa. Minue was killed in the attack.

Famous Ukrainian North Americans

Dr. Joseph V. Charyk, born into a Ukrainian family in Alberta, was an eminent scientist who was appointed head of the Communications Satellite Corporation (COMSAT). Charyk helped create the first communication satellites, providing television coverage around the world. One of these first satellites allowed viewers to see men land on the moon in 1969.

The famous ice hockey player Wayne Gretzky, or "The Great One," traces his origins back to Ukraine through his grandparents, who came to Canada from western Ukraine. Gretzky, who retired from the sport in 1999, holds numerous National Hockey League records for scoring and assists.

Winner of three gold medals at the Sydney 2000 Olympic Games, swimmer Lenny Krayzelburg emigrated to the United States from Odesa, Ukraine, as a teenager.

Ukrainians in North America:
Where and How They Live

Ukrainians in the United States live throughout the country —
from California in the west to New York in the northeast and
Florida in the south. Large Ukrainian communities exist in cities
such as San Francisco, San Diego, Chicago, Detroit, and New
York. In these and other cities, Ukrainian-Americans have
organized community and cultural centers that house exhibits
of Ukrainian art, show Ukrainian films and television programs,
and hold Ukrainian cultural festivals. Many of these cultural
centers are home to Ukrainian dance and folk song groups.

In Canada, the concentration of Ukrainian-Canadians is
high in the provinces of Alberta, Manitoba, and Ontario. The
cities of Calgary, Winnipeg, and Toronto are examples of cities
with thriving Ukrainian communities.

Both Canadian and U.S. immigrant communities work hard
to improve and increase relations between Ukraine and North
America through cultural, educational, and social ties.

Below: **Ukrainian
dance groups are
one of the more visible
examples of Ukrainian
culture present in
North America.**

North Americans in Ukraine

North Americans visit Ukraine today for many reasons. Some are there to do business, while others visit as tourists. The U.S. Peace Corps regularly sends its volunteers to Ukrainian schools to teach English to students.

Many Ukrainian universities have exchange programs with their U.S. counterparts. These programs allow students and scholars from both countries to visit each other for research and teaching purposes. For example, Kharkov National University has a long-standing student and faculty exchange program with several U.S. universities, including the universities of Maine, Southern Maine, Cincinnati, Wisconsin-Green Bay, Missouri-Saint Louis, and California at San Diego.

North American scholars and students come to Ukraine to study Ukrainian history, language, and culture. Ukrainians go to the United States to get experience in business administration, management, and political science. Several universities in both Canada and the United States also offer specialized Ukrainian studies in the country's language, art, and history.

Below: **Ukraine's universities encourage greater ties with their U.S. academic counterparts, allowing students to study in the United States.**

Economic Relations: Exports and Imports

The current developing state of the Ukrainian economy means that the country can sell only a few export commodities to the United States and Canada. One commodity the nation sends North America is steel. The import of steel, however, has previously created tension in the United States.

In 1998, Ukraine and other steel-producing countries around the world were able to sell steel to American plants and factories at prices lower than those charged by American steel companies. This price difference made U.S. steel manufacturers unhappy, and they accused Ukraine and the other steel exporters of deliberately lowering the prices of their goods. Known as "dumping" in the world of business, the low prices allow countries to sell more of their products. Because of the problems caused by cheap steel imports, the U.S. Congress passed a law in 2000 limiting Ukrainian exports of steel to the United States, as well as setting a minimum required price for it.

Besides steel and iron, Ukraine's exports to the United States include aircraft, chemicals, and clothing. Ukraine's imports from the United States include vehicles, machinery, and tobacco.

Above: Cheap steel imports from countries such as Ukraine have angered U.S. steel companies in the past.

A **B** **C** **D**

1

BELARUS

Dnipro

Desna

POLAND

Pripyat

RIVNENS'KA

CHERNIHIVS'KA

VOLYNS'KA

Chernobyl ●
Pripyat ●

Desna

SUM

ZHYTOMYRS'KA

2

KIEV ■

Kiev Reservoir

Koncha-Zaspa ●

Sorochints

● L'viv

L'VIVS'KA

POLTAV

Dnipro

KHMEL'NYTS'KA

TERNOPILS'KA

KYYIVS'KA

SLOVAKIA

Carpathian Mountains

IVANO-
FRANKIVS'KA

Moryntsi ●

CHERKAS'KA

*Kremenchuk
Reservoir*

ZAKARPATS'KA

VINNYTS'KA

3

*Mount Hoverla
(6,762 feet / 2,061 m)*

CHERNIVETS'KA

HUNGARY

Dniester

Southern Buh

KIROVOHRADS'KA

MOLDOVA

MYKOLAYIVS'KA

ODES'KA

Dnipro

4

ROMANIA

Odesa ●

KHERSON

*Perek
Isthm*

KRYM

Danube

UKRAINE

Sevasto

5

BLACK SEA

BULGARIA

86

E　　　　　F

N

	National Boundary
	Oblast Boundary
■	Capital
●	City
	River

RUSSIA

• Kharkov

ishnya　KHARKIVS'KA

oltava

LUHANS'KA

Donets
Basin

PROPETROVS'KA

• Dnipropetrovsk　DONETS'KA

• Zaporizhzhya

Donets'k

ZAPORIZ'KA

ovka
ervoir

iya-Nova
Reserve

SEA OF AZOV

an
sula

nferopol

Mountains

ta

RUSSIA

Askaniya-Nova Nature
　　Reserve E4

Belarus A1–D1
Black Sea C4–F5
Bulgaria A5

Carpathian Mountains
　　A2–B4
Cherkas'ka Oblast
　　C3–D2
Chernihivs'ka Oblast
　　C1–D2
Chernivets'ka Oblast B3
Chernobyl C2
Crimean Mountains E5
Crimean Peninsula
　　D4–E5

Danube River B5–C4
Desna River C2–D1
Dniester River A3–C4
Dnipro River C1–D4
Dnipropetrovsk E3
Dnipropetrovs'ka Oblast
　　D3–E3
Donets Basin F3
Donets'k F3
Donets'ka Oblast E3–F4

Hungary A3

Ivano-Frankivs'ka Oblast
　　A3–B3

Kakhovka Reservoir
　　D4–E3
Kharkivs'ka Oblast
　　E2–F3
Kharkov E2
Khersons'ka Oblast
　　D3–E4
Khmel'nyts'ka Oblast
　　B2–B3
Kiev C2
Kiev Reservoir C2
Kirovohrads'ka Oblast
　　C3–D3
Koncha-Zaspa C2
Kremenchuk Reservoir
　　D2–D3

Kryms'ka Autonomous
　　Republic D4–E5
Kyyivs'ka Oblast C2–D3

Luhans'ka Oblast F2–F3
L'viv A2
L'vivs'ka Oblast A2–B2

Moldova B3–C4
Moryntsi C3
Mount Hoverla A3
Mykolayivs'ka Oblast
　　C3–D4

Odesa C4
Odes'ka Oblast C3–D4
Opishnya E2

Perekop Isthmus D4
Poland A1–A3
Poltava E2
Poltavs'ka Oblast D2–E3
Pripyat C2
Pripyat River A1–C2

Rivnens'ka Oblast
　　B1–B2
Romania A3–C5
Russia D1–F5

Sea of Azov E4–F4
Sevastopol D5
Simferopol E5
Slovakia A2–A3
Sorochintsy D2
Southern Buh River
　　B3–D4
Sums'ka Oblast D1–E2

Ternopils'ka Oblast
　　B2–B3

Vinnyts'ka Oblast B3–C3
Volyns'ka Oblast A1–B2

Yalta E5

Zakarpats'ka Oblast
　　A3–B3
Zaporizhzhya E3
Zaporiz'ka Oblast E3–F4
Zhytomyrs'ka Oblast
　　B2–C2

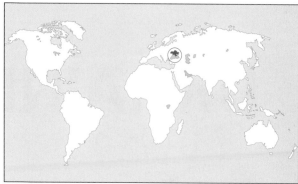

UKRAINE

N

How Is Your Geography?

Learning to identify the main geographical areas and points of a country can be challenging. Although it may seem difficult at first to memorize the locations and spellings of major cities or the names of mountain ranges, rivers, deserts, lakes, and other prominent physical features, the end result of this effort can be very rewarding. Places you previously did not know existed will suddenly come to life when referred to in world news, whether in newspapers, television reports, other books and reference sources, or on the Internet. This knowledge will make you feel a bit closer to the rest of the world, with its fascinating variety of cultures and physical geography.

Used in a classroom setting, the instructor can make duplicates of this map using a copy machine. (PLEASE DO NOT WRITE IN THIS BOOK!) Students can then fill in any requested information on their individual map copies. Used one-on-one, the student can also make copies of the map on a copy machine and use them as a study tool. The student can practice identifying place names and geographical features on his or her own.

Ukraine at a Glance

Official Name   Ukraine

Capital   Kiev

Official Language   Ukrainian

Population   48,760,474 million (July 2001 estimate)

Land Area   233,089 square miles (603,700 square km)

Administrative Divisions   The country is divided into twenty-four administrative regions or oblasti: Cherkas'ka, Chernihivs'ka, Chernivets'ka, Dnipropetrovs'ka, Donets'ka, Ivano-Frankivs'ka, Kharkivs'ka, Khersons'ka, Khmel'nyts'ka, Kirovohrads'ka, Kyyivs'ka, Luhans'ka, L'vivs'ka, Mykolayivs'ka, Odes'ka, Poltavs'ka, Rivnens'ka, Sums'ka, Ternopils'ka, Vinnyts'ka, Volyns'ka, Zakarpats'ka, Zaporiz'ka, Zhytomyrs'ka; and the autonomous republic of Crimea (Kyrms'ka)

Highest Point   Mount Hoverla 6,762 feet (2,061 m)

Major Mountains   Carpathian, Crimean mountain ranges

Main Rivers   Desna, Dniester, Dnipro, Pripyat, Southern Buh

Major Cities   Dnipropetrovsk, Donets'k, Kharkov, Kiev, L'viv, Odesa, Simferopol, Zaporizhzhya

Bordering Countries   Belarus, Hungary, Moldova, Poland, Romania, Russia, Slovakia

Main Religions   Catholicism, Eastern Orthodox, Islam, Judaism

National Holidays   New Year (January 1), Orthodox Christmas (January 7), Women's Day (March 8), Labor Day (May 1–2), Victory Day (May 9), Independence Day (August 24)

Natural Resources   Arable land, coal, graphite, iron ore, kaolin, magnesium, manganese, mercury, natural gas, nickel, oil, salt, sulfur, timber, titanium

Industries   Coal, chemicals, electric power, ferrous and nonferrous metals, machinery and transportation equipment, food processing

Currency   Hryvnia (5.3 hryvnia = U.S. $1 as of 2001)

Opposite: **The Crimean Mountains form an impressive backdrop for Yalta.**

90

Glossary

Ukrainian Vocabulary

babas (BAH-bahs): stone statues of females made by the ancient Scythians.

bandura (bahn-DOO-rah): a modern version of the Ukrainian kobza.

borsch (BOHRSH): beet, cabbage, and tomato soup.

devich vechir (DEH-vich VEH-cheer): a party where the bride bids farewell to her unmarried female friends.

hastronom (hahs-troh-NOHM): a popular type of grocery store where customers have to stand in line to select, pay for, and collect their purchases.

holubtsi (hoh-loob-TSI): a dish made of ground beef and rice wrapped in cabbage leaves.

hopak (hoh-PAHK): a fast-paced Ukrainian folk dance.

horilka (hoh-REEL-kah): a kind of Ukrainian vodka.

hryvnia (HRIV-nyah): the Ukrainian currency introduced in 1996.

kavun (kah-VUN): watermelon.

kobza (KOB-zah): an old stringed musical instrument played by minstrels.

kobzari (kob-zah-REE): traveling, blind, Ukrainian minstrels of ancient times, who played the kobza.

kolyadky (koh-LJAHD-kee): Christmas songs, usually sung by children.

korovai (koh-roh-VAHJ): an elaborately decorated wedding bread.

Kozaks (koh-ZAHKS): peasant/warrior people originating from the banks of the Dnipro River.

kripak (kree-PAHK): serfs; peasants under the control of wealthy landlords.

maidan (maj-DAN): square; place for public gathering

oblasti (OB-lahs-tee): the twenty-four administrative regions of Ukraine.

ogorod (oh-goh-ROHD): a plot of land, usually adjacent to a country house, where Ukrainians grow vegetables.

oseledets (oh-seh-LEH-dehts): a clump of hair left on a Kozak's shaved head.

pysanka (PEA-sahn-kah): an Easter egg decorated with designs that have special meanings.

rushnyk (roosh-NIHK): an embroidered linen towel used in engagement and wedding ceremonies.

sad (SAHD): a plot of land, usually found in villages, used to grow fruits.

sharovary (shah-roh-VAH-reeh): loose, usually red or crimson pants that are part of a man's folk costume.

sich (SEECH): a Kozak warrior fortress built from logs.

starosty (STAH-rohs-tee): well-respected villagers who accompany the prospective groom to the bride's parents' house to propose marriage.

tryzub (tree-ZOOB): the trident, an ancient emblem of Ukraine.

varenyky (vah-REH-nee-kee): crescent-shaped dough dumplings that contain various fillings.

veche (VAY-chay): a decision-making council of elders that existed during the reign of the Kievan Rus kingdom.

English Vocabulary

annexed: added another state or territory to an existing nation.

assassinated: killed someone, usually a politically prominent person, suddenly or secretively.

autonomous republic: a part of a country that is allowed to make its own laws.

boycott (n): the act of not buying or using certain goods or services, often as a way of protest.

breadbasket: an area that produces large amounts of grain.

canonized: declared a saint.

celestial: related to the sky.

choreographic: relating to the planned movements, steps, and patterns of a dance.

collectivization: the organization of an industry into a system owned and controlled by the people as a group.

compote: fruit cooked or stewed in syrup, often served as a dessert.

concessions: changes made by a government or controlling authority to satisfy protests and complaints.

cradle: a place of origins; birthplace.

Cyrillic: an alphabet derived from Greek symbols used in writing Ukrainian and other Slavic languages.

czar: a Russian emperor.

defiantly: showing resistance to authority or an opposing force.

dynamics: pattern or history of growth, change, and development.

ethnic: relating to a group that shares a common culture, religion, or language.

exiled: removed from one's own country, usually by force.

guerrilla: a member of a small independent band of soldiers that harasses the enemy by surprise raids.

imperial: related to the rule of an empire.

inflation: a steady increase in the price of goods in a country, often resulting in the loss of value of its currency.

isthmus: a narrow strip of land, surrounded by water, connecting two land masses.

medieval: related to the Middle Ages; a period in European history from about 500 to 1500.

mercenary: working or acting solely for money; a soldier hired to serve in a foreign army.

minstrels: musicians, singers, or poets, often associated with medieval times.

modernism: a literary movement of the early twentieth century that emphasizes a break from the past to create forms of expression.

nationalism: devotion to one's nation.

nomadic: without a permanent home; moving around in search of food.

peasants: members of a class of farmers or laborers of a low social rank.

peninsula: land surrounded by water on three sides.

sarcophagus: a stone coffin for ancient Egyptian mummies; the concrete casing built to cover the exploded Chernobyl nuclear reactor.

scouts: persons sent out to discover talent.

serfs: farmworkers who cannot leave the land on which they work and are under the control of a landlord.

subsidizing: giving financial aid to a company, usually to lower prices on the company's products for the consumer.

More Books to Read

Chernobyl Nuclear Disaster. Great Disasters: Reforms and Ramifications series. Kristine Brennan (Chelsea House)

Thousands of Roads: A Memoir of a Young Woman's Life in the Ukrainian Underground During and After World War II. Maria Savchyn Pyskir (McFarland and Company)

Treasury of Ukrainian Love: Poems, Quotations & Proverbs in Ukrainian and English. Hélène Turkewicz-Sanko (Hippecrene Books)

Simply Ukraine. Tania D'Avignon (Artex Management)

Ukraine. Cultures of the World series. Volodymyr Bassis (Benchmark Books)

Ukraine. Modern Nations of the World: Former Soviet Republics series. Laurel Corona (Lucent Books)

Ukraine: A New Independence. Exploring Cultures of the World series. Rebecca Clay (Benchmark Books)

Ukrainian Folk Tales. Marie H. Bloch (Hippocrene Books)

The Ukrainian Icon. 11th to 18th Centuries. Liudmilla Milyaeva (Parkstone Press)

Videos

Golden Kiev. (Universe Productions)

Ukrainian Journey. (Universe Productions)

Video Visits – Ukraine: Ancient Crossroads, Modern Dreams. (IVN Entertainment)

Web Sites

www.brama.com

www.infoukes.com/culture/traditions

www.uazone.net

www.ukraine.org

www.ukrania.com

Due to the dynamic nature of the Internet, some web sites stay current longer than others. To find additional web sites, use a reliable search engine with one or more of the following keywords to help you locate information about Ukraine. Keywords: *Chernobyl, Crimea, Kievan Rus,* kobzari, Kozaks, pysanka, *Taras Shevchenko,* varenyky.

Index